GRAPHIC NONFICTION

CHRISTOPHER COLUMBUS

THE LIFE OF A MASTER NAVIGATOR AND EXPLORER

by
DAVID WEST & J

illustrated
ROSS WATTON

BOOK HOUSE

Designed and produced by
David West 👥 Children's Books,
7 Princeton Court,
55 Felsham Road,
London, SW15 1AZ

Editor: Gail Bushnell
Photo Research: Carlotta Cooper

Photo credits:
Pages 5, 7, 44 (top), 45 – Mary Evans Picture Library
Pages 6 (top), 44 (left & bottom) – The Culture Archive

First published in 2005 by **Book House**,
an imprint of **The Salariya Book Company Ltd**
25 Marlborough Place, Brighton BN1 1UB

Please visit the Salariya Book Company at:
www.salariya.com

HB ISBN 1 905087 17 9
PB ISBN 1 905087 18 7

Visit our website at **www.book-house.co.uk** for free electronic versions of:
You wouldn't want to be an Egyptian Mummy!
You wouldn't want to be a Roman Gladiator!
Avoid joining Shackleton's Polar Expedition!
Avoid sailing on a 19th century Whaling Ship!

Due to the changing nature of internet links, the Salariya Book Company has
developed an online list of websites related to the subject of this book. This site is
updated regularly. Please use this link to access the list:
http://www.book-house.co.uk/gnf/columbus

A catalogue record for this book is available from the British Library.

Printed on paper from sustainable forests.

Manufactured in China.

CONTENTS

WHO'S WHO

Christopher Columbus (1451-1506) Genoese sailor and navigator who was the first European to explore what is now the West Indies. He made four voyages from 1492-1504. He called himself Cristobal Colón after he settled in Spain in 1485.

Bartolomeo Columbus (c. 1452-1514) One of Christopher's brothers, Bartolomeo was his lifelong supporter and took part in each voyage, except the first.

Diego Columbus (c. 1468-1515) Christopher's youngest brother, Diego, took part in the second and third voyages. He later became a priest.

Felipa Moniz de Perestrello (*dates unknown*) Felipa married Christopher in about 1478. Felipa died before Christopher left Portugal in 1485.

Fernando Colón (1488-1539) The son of Christopher and Beatriz Enríquez de Arana, Fernando went on his father's fourth voyage. He later wrote Christopher's life story.

Martín Alonso Pinzón (c. 1442-1493) Head of a seafaring family from Palos, Spain. He captained the *Pinta* on the first voyage. His brother, Vicente Yáñez Pinzón, commanded the *Niña* on the same voyage.

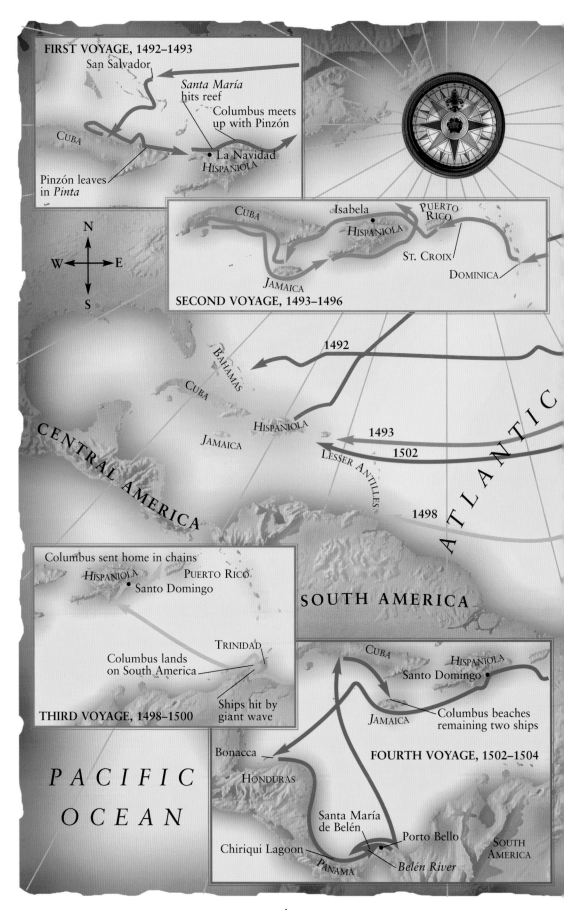

FIRST VOYAGE, 1492–1493

San Salvador

Santa María hits reef

Columbus meets up with Pinzón

CUBA

• La Navidad

HISPANIOLA

Pinzón leaves in *Pinta*

SECOND VOYAGE, 1493–1496

CUBA

Isabela

HISPANIOLA

PUERTO RICO

St. CROIX

DOMINICA

JAMAICA

N
W — E
S

1492

BAHAMAS

CUBA

JAMAICA

HISPANIOLA

LESSER ANTILLES

1493

1502

1498

CENTRAL AMERICA

ATLANTIC

SOUTH AMERICA

THIRD VOYAGE, 1498–1500

Columbus sent home in chains

HISPANIOLA

PUERTO RICO

• Santo Domingo

TRINIDAD

Columbus lands on South America

Ships hit by giant wave

PACIFIC

OCEAN

FOURTH VOYAGE, 1502–1504

CUBA

HISPANIOLA

Santo Domingo •

Columbus beaches remaining two ships

JAMAICA

Bonacca

HONDURAS

Santa María de Belén

Porto Bello

Chiriqui Lagoon

PANAMA

Belén River

SOUTH AMERICA

THE FOUR VOYAGES

In 1492, explorer Christopher Columbus set sail from Spain and headed west into unknown seas. It was the first of his four voyages to the regions we now call the West Indies and Central and South America.

ENGLAND

FRANCE

ITALY

PORTUGAL

SPAIN

MEDITERRANEAN SEA

1493

AZORES

Lisbon

Lagos

Palos

Cadiz

OCEAN

MADEIRA ISLANDS

Gomera

CANARY ISLANDS

AFRICA

A Small World
Drawn in 1492, this map (left) shows what Europeans believed the world looked like before Columbus's voyages. The Atlantic Ocean was thought to be narrower than it actually is and the Americas and the Pacific Ocean are both missing.

The Riches of the Indies

Before Columbus's voyages, Europeans knew nothing of the Americas. They did know that there were vast lands to the east of Europe. They did not know exactly where the lands were. They called the region the Indies and believed it was rich in gold. Eastern products such as silks and spices were highly valued in Europe. Fortunes could be made trading in them. At the time, however, trade routes to the east were mainly over land. The only known water routes were via the Mediterranean Sea. These land and sea routes went through dangerous Muslim lands. The Muslim world and Christian Europe had been enemies for hundreds of years. Europeans needed to discover a new route to the Indies. However, none of their sailors had ever travelled around the tip of Africa, nor did any living Europeans know of any route across the Atlantic Ocean.

EXPLORERS & SAILORS

*L*ike other Europeans of his time,
Columbus meant all eastern lands when
he talked of the Indies – from India and
China to Japan and Indonesia. Few
Europeans had actually travelled there.
Most of their ideas about the Indies were
based on the travels of Marco Polo.

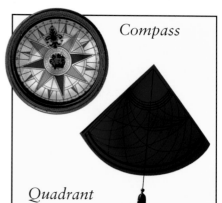

Compass

Quadrant

THE TRAVELS OF MARCO POLO

The Italian trader, Marco Polo, set out on
an extraordinary overland voyage to China
in 1271. On his return 24 years later, he
wrote a book that made his travels famous
throughout Europe. Polo told astonishing
tales of the wealthy and marvellous cities
of China, which he called Cathay, and
Cipango, or Japan. The book inspired
countless explorers. Columbus's copy was
one of his most treasured possessions.

NAVIGATIONAL TOOLS
*As well as a compass,
Columbus had a device
called a quadrant to help
him work out his north-
south position from the
stars. Quadrants were
unreliable because they
were hard to hold steady
enough to read on a
moving ship.*

SAILING INTO THE UNKNOWN

When sailors set off into the Atlantic Ocean
in search of the Indies in the sixteenth
century, they were heading into the unknown. They were brave men.
Powered by the wind, their wooden sailing ships were often at the mercy
of the weather. Maps of the world were mainly guesswork. Apart from a
compass, navigators had few tools. Compasses can tell you the direction
you are heading in, but they cannot tell you how far you are to the north,
south, east, or west. To work out where they were, navigators relied

chiefly on the position of
the stars in the
night sky.

A ROUND WORLD
*In the fifteenth century,
mapmakers were able
to make globes. At that
time, most educated
Europeans thought the
Earth was round. Yet
because no one had ever
sailed around the world,
they had no real proof.*

XPO FERENS.

CHRISTOPHER COLUMBUS

Columbus's home city was the busy port of Genoa, Italy. His father, Domenico, was a wool weaver. His mother, Susanna Fontanarossa, was the daughter of a weaver. Born in 1451, Christopher was their first child. Two of his younger brothers, Bartolomeo and Diego, grew up to share his fascination with exploration and travelled with him on some of his voyages. Another brother, Giovanni, died young, and little is known of his sister, Bianchinetta. Not much is known about Christopher's schooling, although he probably learned to read and write at a young age. We do know that his school days were over by his early teens. This was when he first went to sea to begin his lifelong career as a sailor, navigator, and explorer.

ON A MISSION
After his first voyage, Columbus began using this signature. It says Christopher, or "Christ bearer", in Greek and Latin. One of the aims of his travels was to convert the natives of the Indies to Christianity.

THE PORT OF GENOA
This picture shows the street in Genoa where Columbus was born. Columbus grew up surrounded by sailors and tales of exploring, because Genoa was one of Europe's largest trading centres. Genoese ships sailed to ports all over the Mediterranean, carrying everything from woolen cloth to exotic silks and spices.

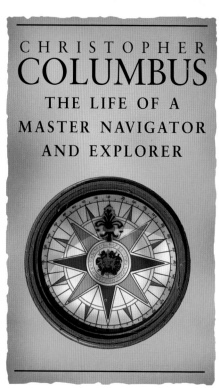

CHRISTOPHER COLUMBUS

THE LIFE OF A MASTER NAVIGATOR AND EXPLORER

THE YEAR WAS 1476. I HAD TAKEN A JOB AS A COMMON SAILOR WITH A GENOESE TRADING FLEET. WE WERE OFF PORTUGAL'S SOUTHERN COAST WHEN THE ENEMY CAME INTO SIGHT.

FRENCH PRIVATEERS!*

MAN THE GUNS!

*PRIVATEERS WERE PRIVATELY OWNED SHIPS PAID TO BACK UP GOVERNMENT NAVIES IN TIMES OF WAR. THEY ROBBED OR SANK ENEMY TRADING SHIPS.

BY SAN FERNANDO. THEY LOOK LIKE THEY MEAN BUSINESS.

THE BATTLE **RAGED** FOR MANY **HOURS.**

JUMP FOR IT! WE'RE SINKING!

GLUURGH

IT MUST BE SIX MILES TO SHORE.

HERE – GET HIS LEGS.

WH–WHERE AM I?

NEAR LAGOS. WHAT'S YOUR NAME?

CHRISTOPHER COLUMBUS.

I WAS TREATED WITH GREAT KINDNESS.

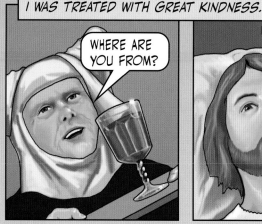

WHERE ARE YOU FROM?

GENOA.

YOU SHOULD MAKE YOUR WAY TO THE PORT OF LISBON. MANY GENOESE LIVE THERE.

WHEN I WAS WELL ENOUGH TO TRAVEL, I HEADED NORTH FOR LISBON.

SOON I WAS JOINED BY MY YOUNGER BROTHER BARTOLOMEO.

GOOD TO SEE YOU, BROTHER.

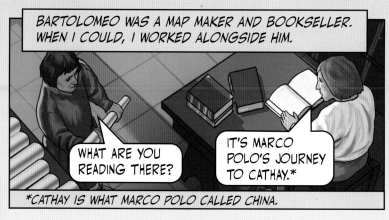

BARTOLOMEO WAS A MAP MAKER AND BOOKSELLER. WHEN I COULD, I WORKED ALONGSIDE HIM.

WHAT ARE YOU READING THERE?

IT'S MARCO POLO'S JOURNEY TO CATHAY.*

*CATHAY IS WHAT MARCO POLO CALLED CHINA.

WE ALSO BEGAN STUDYING LATIN AND OTHER LANGUAGES.

MY GREAT LOVE WAS THE **SEA**, THOUGH, AND I JOINED AS MANY TRADING VOYAGES AS I COULD.

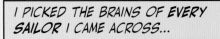

I PICKED THE BRAINS OF **EVERY SAILOR** I CAME ACROSS...

A BEAUTIFUL MERMAID SAVED MY SHIP. HER SONG WARNED US TO STEER CLEAR OF THE ROCKS.

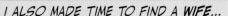

I ALSO MADE TIME TO FIND A **WIFE**...

WON'T YOU TELL ME YOUR NAME, MY ANGEL?

DOÑA FELIPA MONIZ DE PERESTRELLO.

THE LADY BELONGS TO ONE OF PORTUGAL'S LEADING NOBLE FAMILIES.

TELL ME ABOUT YOUR FAMILY.

MY FATHER WAS GOVERNOR OF PORTO SANTO IN THE MADEIRA ISLANDS. HE DIED A FEW YEARS AGO. WHAT ABOUT **YOURS?**

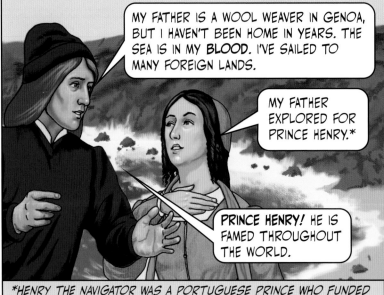

MY FATHER IS A WOOL WEAVER IN GENOA, BUT I HAVEN'T BEEN HOME IN YEARS. THE SEA IS IN MY **BLOOD**. I'VE SAILED TO MANY FOREIGN LANDS.

MY FATHER EXPLORED FOR PRINCE HENRY.*

PRINCE HENRY! HE IS FAMED THROUGHOUT THE WORLD.

BY 1479, WE WERE MAN AND WIFE.

*HENRY THE NAVIGATOR WAS A PORTUGUESE PRINCE WHO FUNDED MANY VOYAGES OF EXPLORATION ALONG THE WEST AFRICAN COAST.

WE LIVED IN PORTO SANTO AT FIRST.

MY BROTHER IS TO FOLLOW IN OUR FATHER'S FOOTSTEPS AS GOVERNOR OF THE ISLAND.

OUR SON WAS BORN THERE.

WE'LL NAME HIM **DIEGO**, AFTER MY BROTHER.

SOON AFTER, WE MOVED TO MADEIRA.

CHRISTOPHER, YOU MIGHT LIKE THESE CHARTS AND LETTERS OF MY LATE HUSBAND'S.

MY MOTHER-IN-LAW GAVE ME HER HUSBAND'S PAPERS.

THERE'S A WEALTH OF INFORMATION HERE — **MAPS** AND **INTERVIEWS** WITH EXPLORERS!

BUT MY HAPPINESS WAS SHORT-LIVED. WITHIN MONTHS, FELIPA WAS **DEAD**. I WAS **HEARTBROKEN**.

I FILLED MY TIME WITH MORE VOYAGES. BY 1483, I HAD VISITED GUINEA ON THE COAST OF WEST AFRICA. IT WAS HERE THAT I LEARNED OF A STRONG OCEAN CURRENT THAT **FLOWED WEST** FROM THE CANARY ISLANDS.

CATHAY LIES TO THE WEST. I'M **SURE** OF IT.

11

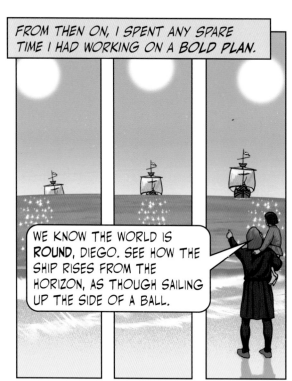

FROM THEN ON, I SPENT ANY SPARE TIME I HAD WORKING ON A **BOLD PLAN.**

WE KNOW THE WORLD IS **ROUND**, DIEGO. SEE HOW THE SHIP RISES FROM THE HORIZON, AS THOUGH SAILING UP THE SIDE OF A BALL.

MARCO POLO PUTS CATHAY ON THE SAME **LATITUDE** AS THE CANARY ISLANDS, OFF THE COAST OF AFRICA.*

*LATITUDES ARE EAST-WEST LINES DRAWN ON MAPS OF THE EARTH.

TOSCANELLI BELIEVES YOU CAN REACH THE EAST BY SAILING **WEST!***

*PAOLO TOSCANELLI OF FLORENCE, ITALY, WAS A GEOGRAPHER.

IF GOD HAS A PURPOSE IN MIND FOR ME...

...IT IS TO FIND A **WESTERN SEA ROUTE** TO CATHAY!

MOST PEOPLE BELIEVED THAT THERE WAS ONLY ONE WAY TO GET TO CATHAY, OR CHINA, AND THE INDIES – BY TRAVELLING **EAST.** CHRISTOPHER NEEDED ROYAL BACKING TO HELP **FUND** HIS VOYAGE OF EXPLORATION AND TO **LAY CLAIM** TO ANY NEW LANDS HE DISCOVERED. LUCKILY, FELIPA'S FAMILY HAD CONNECTIONS AT THE PORTUGUESE COURT. THE PORTUGUESE KING, JOHN II, WAS INTERESTED IN EXPLORING THE ATLANTIC OCEAN.

IN 1484, THE KING OF PORTUGAL WAS KIND ENOUGH TO GRANT ME AN INTERVIEW...

YOUR HIGHNESS, MY PLAN IS TO FIND A ROUTE TO THE INDIES – BY SAILING **WEST** ACROSS THE ATLANTIC!

YES, YES, MOST **INTERESTING.** I WILL PUT IT TO MY ADVISERS.

BUT MY HOPES WERE DASHED...

THEY'VE TURNED DOWN MY PLAN.

WHAT? WHY?

THEY SAY MY MEASUREMENTS ARE **WRONG** AND THAT THE OCEAN IS TOO WIDE TO SAIL ACROSS.* BAH!

*CHRISTOPHER'S MEASUREMENTS **WERE** WRONG. HE HAD MADE A MISTAKE IN HIS MATHS!

I LEFT PORTUGAL FOR SPAIN SOON AFTER, TAKING MY YOUNG SON, DIEGO, WITH ME.

PORTUGAL'S LOSS WILL BE SPAIN'S **GAIN**.

WE REACHED A MONASTERY NEAR THE SPANISH TOWN OF HUELVA. RELATIVES OF MY LATE WIFE LIVED THERE.

GREETINGS, FRIAR. CAN YOU SPARE A LITTLE BREAD AND WATER FOR TWO WEARY TRAVELLERS?

THE FRIARS AGREED TO CARE FOR DIEGO. SOME OF THEM SUPPORTED MY PLAN TO FIND A WESTERN SEA ROUTE.

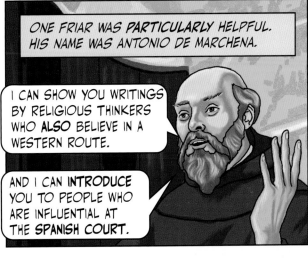

ONE FRIAR WAS **PARTICULARLY** HELPFUL. HIS NAME WAS ANTONIO DE MARCHENA.

I CAN SHOW YOU WRITINGS BY RELIGIOUS THINKERS WHO **ALSO** BELIEVE IN A WESTERN ROUTE.

AND I CAN **INTRODUCE** YOU TO PEOPLE WHO ARE INFLUENTIAL AT THE **SPANISH COURT**.

SOMETIME LATER I MET THE DUKE OF MEDINA SIDONIA...

I WILL SEE WHAT I CAN DO TO HELP YOU.

IT WAS ABOUT THIS TIME THAT I MET TWO WELL-RESPECTED LOCAL SEA CAPTAINS, THE BROTHERS MARTÍN ALONSO PINZÓN AND VICENTE YÁÑEZ PINZÓN.

IN 1486, I WAS LUCKY ENOUGH TO BE GRANTED A MEETING WITH THE SPANISH RULERS, KING FERDINAND AND QUEEN ISABELLA. THE QUEEN WAS TO BECOME A LIFELONG SUPPORTER.

IT IS MOST **GRACIOUS** OF YOU TO SEE ME.

QUEEN ISABELLA ARRANGED FOR HER ADVISERS TO LOOK INTO MY PLANS.

BUT THE ADVISERS WERE IN **NO HURRY** TO MAKE A DECISION...

WE NEED TO CHECK THIS CAREFULLY.

YES. I HAVE **MANY QUESTIONS** TO ASK COLUMBUS.

IN FACT, SPAIN HAD LITTLE **TIME OR MONEY** TO GIVE TO EXPLORERS. THE NATION WAS TOO BUSY FIGHTING THE **MOORS** – MUSLIMS FROM NORTH AFRICA WHO HAD INVADED SPAIN IN THE EARLY 700S. BY THE 1480S, ONLY GRANADA, IN SOUTHERN SPAIN, WAS STILL RULED BY THE MOORS. FERDINAND AND ISABELLA WERE BATTLING TO **DRIVE** THEM OUT.

THE QUEEN GAVE ME A SMALL WAGE. I FILLED MY TIME DOING RESEARCH. MANY MONTHS PASSED.

SURELY I WILL HEAR FROM THE QUEEN'S ADVISERS **SOON**.

FORTUNATELY, MY HOME LIFE WAS HAPPY. IN 1488, MY COMPANION, BEATRIZ ENRÍQUEZ DE ARANA, GAVE BIRTH TO OUR SON, FERNANDO.

THE QUEEN'S ADVISERS STILL HAD NOT REACHED A DECISION. SO I ASKED BARTOLOMEO TO SEEK HELP **ABROAD**...

PERHAPS THE RULERS OF ENGLAND OR FRANCE MIGHT SUPPORT MY PLANS?

BUT **NEITHER** NATION WOULD HELP. IN DECEMBER 1488, THERE WAS **MORE** BAD NEWS.

HAVE YOU HEARD ABOUT BARTOLOMEO DIAS?

YES, HE'S FOUND A SEA ROUTE **AROUND AFRICA** – THE WAY **EAST** IS OPEN. **NO ONE** WILL BE INTERESTED IN A **WESTERN ROUTE** NOW.

FINALLY, IN LATE 1490, THE QUEEN'S ADVISERS MADE THEIR DECISION. **IT WAS "NO".** I WENT TO THE MONASTERY TO GET DIEGO.

THEY, TOO, BELIEVE THE OCEAN IS TOO WIDE. **ALL IS LOST!** I'M LEAVING SPAIN, FRIAR.

NO, WAIT. I WILL ASK THE QUEEN FOR ONE LAST MEETING.

I MET WITH THE KING AND QUEEN IN FALL 1491. THEY WERE PREPARING A **MAJOR ATTACK** ON THE MOORS.

...AND I ALSO ASK TO BE GIVEN POSITIONS OF RANK IF MY VOYAGE IS A SUCCESS.

IN JANUARY 1492, FERDINAND AND ISABELLA'S ARMY CONQUERED GRANADA AND DROVE OUT THE MOORS.

WHERE ARE YOU GOING, CHRISTOPHER? WON'T YOU JOIN THE CELEBRATIONS?

THEY'VE TURNED ME DOWN **AGAIN!**

A FRIEND AT THE SPANISH COURT MADE A **FINAL PLEA** ON MY BEHALF...

YOUR MAJESTIES, THE VOYAGE IS AN OPPORTUNITY **NOT** TO BE MISSED.

FINALLY, MY PATIENCE WAS REWARDED...

WAIT, CHRISTOPHER, WAIT! ALL IS WELL. THEIR MAJESTIES HAVE CHANGED THEIR MINDS!

IF MY VOYAGE WAS SUCCESSFUL, FERDINAND AND ISABELLA PROMISED TO GIVE ME A SHARE IN THE **RICHES** THAT I BROUGHT BACK FROM THE INDIES. I WAS ALSO TO BE MADE **ADMIRAL** OF THE OCEAN AND **GOVERNOR** OF THE INDIES.

MY THREE SHIPS SET SAIL FROM THE SPANISH PORT OF PALOS ON 3RD AUGUST, 1492. I WAS ON THE **SANTA MARIA**. THE **PINTA** WAS COMMANDED BY MARTIN PINZÓN AND THE **NIÑA** BY HIS BROTHER, VICENTE PINZÓN. TOGETHER, WE HAD A CREW OF ABOUT 90 EXPERIENCED SAILORS.

WE HEADED SOUTH TO THE CANARY ISLANDS.

THE PINTA IS SIGNALLING THAT SHE'S IN TROUBLE.

THERE WAS A PROBLEM WITH THE PINTA'S STEERING GEAR.

THE RUDDER HAS JUMPED OUT OF ITS HOLDINGS.

DO YOUR BEST TO FIX IT, THEN FOLLOW US AS **QUICKLY** AS YOU CAN MANAGE.

ON 12TH AUGUST, THE SANTA MARIA AND THE NIÑA REACHED GOMERA, ONE OF THE CANARY ISLANDS.

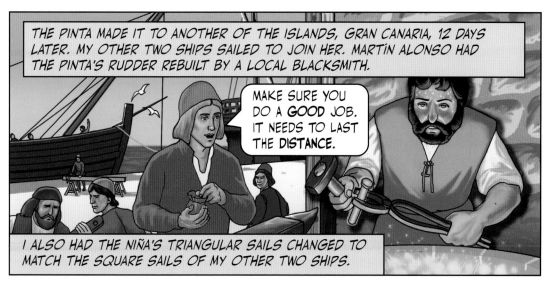

THE PINTA MADE IT TO ANOTHER OF THE ISLANDS, GRAN CANARIA, 12 DAYS LATER. MY OTHER TWO SHIPS SAILED TO JOIN HER. MARTÍN ALONSO HAD THE PINTA'S RUDDER REBUILT BY A LOCAL BLACKSMITH.

MAKE SURE YOU DO A **GOOD** JOB. IT NEEDS TO LAST THE **DISTANCE**.

I ALSO HAD THE NIÑA'S TRIANGULAR SAILS CHANGED TO MATCH THE SQUARE SAILS OF MY OTHER TWO SHIPS.

WE ALL RETURNED TO GOMERA, WHERE I MET WITH THE RULER, THE BEAUTIFUL DOÑA BEATRIZ DE PERAZA.

WELCOME! MY HOME IS YOUR HOME.

NEWS ARRIVED THAT KING JOHN II OF PORTUGAL HAD SENT THREE SHIPS TO **CHASE US**.

THEY MAY TRY TO STOP US FROM SAILING INTO THEIR WATERS.*

*THE PORTUGUESE HAD LAID CLAIM TO THE OCEAN SOUTHWEST OF THE CANARIES.

MY SHIPS WERE STOCKED WITH ENOUGH SUPPLIES TO LAST A YEAR. ON 6TH SEPTEMBER, I ATTENDED MASS, THEN SAID FAREWELL TO DOÑA BEATRIZ.

MAY YOUR MISSION BE **SUCCESSFUL**.

THANK YOU FOR YOUR **KINDNESS**.

WE SAILED DUE WEST. HELPED BY FAVOURABLE WINDS AND CURRENTS, WE MADE GOOD TIME.

STEER DUE WEST!

WE SAW NO SIGN OF THE PORTUGUESE.

WE WERE OUT OF SIGHT OF LAND, SAILING INTO **UNKNOWN** WATERS. BUT AFTER ALL MY YEARS AT SEA, **NAVIGATION** WAS ALMOST SECOND NATURE TO ME.

I RECORDED OUR ROUTE ON MY CHARTS. MY TOOLS FOR NAVIGATION WERE...

...AN **HOURGLASS**,...

...A **QUADRANT**, AND A **COMPASS**.

I USED THE STARS AT **NIGHT**...

...AND THE SUN AT **MIDDAY** TO RECORD OUR POSITION.

TO JUDGE OUR SPEED AND HOW FAR WE TRAVELLED EACH DAY...

...I COUNTED THE TIME IT TOOK A FLOATING OBJECT TO TRAVEL THE LENGTH OF THE SHIP.

THE MEN ATE ONE HOT MEAL A DAY, COOKED ON DECK OVER AN OPEN FIREBOX. CHICKPEAS AND LENTILS WERE STEWED UP, SOMETIMES WITH SALTED MEAT OR FISH.*

BURP

EURPH

*TO STOP THEM FROM ROTTING, FISH AND MEAT WERE SOAKED IN SALT AND PUT IN BARRELS.

SUNRISE SHOWED US TO BE SAILING UP THE EAST COAST OF A SMALL ISLAND...

IT'S BEAUTIFUL!

LOOK – MERMAIDS!*

*SEA MAMMALS CALLED MANATEES WERE OFTEN MISTAKEN FOR MERMAIDS BY SAILORS.

THE ISLAND WAS ALMOST SURROUNDED BY *DANGEROUS* REEFS, BUT WE FOUND A GAP.

MY THREE SHIPS WEIGHED ANCHOR NEAR THE SHORE.

KERSPLOOSH

I NAME THIS ISLAND SAN SALVADOR, AND I CLAIM IT IN THE NAME OF FERDINAND AND ISABELLA OF SPAIN.*

*NO ONE TODAY IS CERTAIN WHICH ISLAND THIS WAS, BUT IT WAS PROBABLY IN THE BAHAMAS. COLUMBUS BELIEVED IT WAS ONE OF THE MANY ISLANDS EAST OF CIPANGO, OR JAPAN.

WE NAMED THE NATIVES THE TAÍNOS.* TO SHOW OUR FRIENDSHIP, WE GAVE THEM BEADS AND OTHER TRINKETS. THEY WERE **GENTLE** AND SHOWED NO FEAR – EVEN OF OUR **WEAPONS**.

*SOON ALL NATIVES IN THE REGION WERE CALLED "INDIANS", BECAUSE THE EUROPEANS BELIEVED THEY HAD REACHED THE INDIES.

THEY WEAR **GOLD PIECES** IN THEIR NOSES!

WE USED SIGN LANGUAGE TO TALK AND LEARNED OF MORE ISLANDS TO THE WEST.

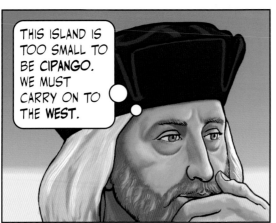

THIS ISLAND IS TOO SMALL TO BE **CIPANGO**. WE MUST CARRY ON TO THE **WEST**.

I GAVE THE ORDER TO SET SAIL AGAIN. WE **CAPTURED** A FEW TAÍNOS TO GUIDE US AND TO TRAIN AS **INTERPRETERS**.

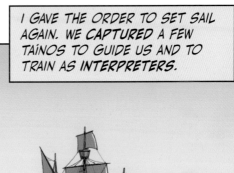

WE FOUND MANY NEW ISLANDS AND CLAIMED THEM FOR SPAIN. BUT NONE OF THEM WERE BIG ENOUGH TO BE CIPANGO.

THE PLANTS AND ANIMALS OF THESE BEAUTIFUL ISLANDS ARE LIKE **NOTHING** I'VE EVER SEEN BEFORE.

IN LATE OCTOBER 1492, I WAS SURE I HAD REACHED MY JOURNEY'S END.

THEY TALK OF COLBA.* THEY SAY IT IS A VERY BIG ISLAND, WITH MUCH GOLD.

IT MUST BE CIPANGO!

*COLBA WAS THE NATIVE WORD FOR THE ISLAND THE SPANISH LATER NAMED CUBA.

WE LANDED IN MANY PLACES AND EVEN EXPLORED INLAND. BUT MARCO POLO HAD TALKED OF CIPANGO'S GOLD-ROOFED CITIES AND ELEGANT NOBLES – AND WE FOUND **NO TRACE** OF THEM.

IT IS TOO **BIG** TO BE AN ISLAND.

PERHAPS IT IS NOT CIPANGO, BUT THE **MAINLAND OF CATHAY?***

*COLUMBUS ENDED UP BELIEVING THAT CUBA WAS PART OF CATHAY, OR CHINA.

WE CARRIED ON WITH OUR SEARCH. IN SOME PLACES, THE TAÍNOS BECAME **FEARFUL**.

WHAT ARE THEY SO FRIGHTENED OF?

THEY TALK OF NATIVES CALLED CARIBS – CANNIBALS WHO WILL **EAT US!**

ALTHOUGH WE DID NOT FIND CANNIBALS, WE MADE OTHER INTERESTING DISCOVERIES – DOGS THAT DO NOT BARK AND HANGING BEDS!

WHAT ARE THE DOGS USED FOR?

THE NATIVES EAT THEM.

THESE BEDS GIVE ME AN IDEA...

BUT THERE WAS NO GOLD. THE PINTA'S CAPTAIN, MARTÍN PINZÓN, GREW **IMPATIENT**.

WE SHOULD BE LOOKING FOR GOLD!

IN NOVEMBER, HE SAILED AWAY IN THE PINTA TO CARRY OUT **HIS OWN** SEARCH FOR THE RICHES OF THE INDIES.

CURSE HIM! HE THINKS OF NOTHING BUT **GOLD**.

TAKING THE SANTA MARÍA AND THE NIÑA, I ALSO LEFT CATHAY TO HUNT FOR GOLD.

ON 7TH DECEMBER 1492, WE ANCHORED OFF ANOTHER ISLAND.

I NAME THIS LAND LA ISLA ESPAÑOLA.*

*TODAY CALLED HISPANIOLA, IT IS DIVIDED INTO HAITI AND THE DOMINICAN REPUBLIC.

AT LAST WE HAD FOUND NATIVES WHO SEEMED RICH.

THEY WEAR SO MUCH GOLD JEWELLERY!

WE EXPLORED THE COAST. I MET A TAÍNOS KING CALLED GUACANAGARI AND INVITED HIM ON BOARD THE SANTA MARÍA.

HE SAYS THERE IS MUCH GOLD ON NEARBY ISLANDS.

ON CHRISTMAS EVE, WE SET OFF TO FIND THE ISLANDS OF GOLD. BUT LATE THAT NIGHT, DISASTER STRUCK...

...THE SANTA MARÍA HIT A REEF!

AWAKE! AWAKE!

WE HAD TIME TO ESCAPE TO THE NIÑA, BUT THE SANTA MARÍA WAS TOO BADLY DAMAGED TO REPAIR. WHEN DAYLIGHT CAME, WE FERRIED ALL THE SUPPLIES WE COULD SAVE FROM HER TO THE NIÑA.

THE NIÑA WAS TOO SMALL TO CARRY ALL MY MEN HOME TO SPAIN. I DECIDED TO LEAVE SOME MEN BEHIND. WE BUILT A **FORT**, WHICH I NAMED LA NAVIDAD.

WE WILL RETURN WITHIN A YEAR.

DON'T WORRY. THE NATIVES ARE **FRIENDLY** AND THE ISLAND IS **RICH** IN FOOD AND GOLD.

THE FORT WAS **FLOODED** WITH TAÍNOS VISITORS. THEY WANTED TO SWAP THEIR GOLD FOR TRINKETS SUCH AS BELLS.

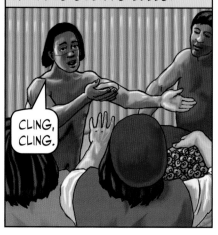

CLING, CLING.

ON 4TH JANUARY 1493, THE NIÑA SET SAIL FOR SPAIN. WE HEADED SOUTHEAST, HUGGING THE COASTLINE.

WE TOOK SOME OF THE NATIVES WE HAD CAPTURED WITH US.

A COUPLE OF DAYS LATER, WE **SIGHTED** THE PINTA. MARTÍN PINZÓN BOARDED OUR SHIP AND TRIED TO **MAKE UP** WITH ME.

I HEARD OF YOUR SHIPWRECK AND **HURRIED** TO HELP.

WE MAY HAVE LOST A SHIP, BUT OUR HOLD IS **FULL OF GOLD!**

WE FOUND **YET MORE** GOLD WHEN WE STOPPED TO TAKE ON RIVER WATER.

THERE ARE PEA-SIZED LUMPS OF GOLD!

AT ANOTHER LANDING, WE SAW **ARMED NATIVES** WHO DID NOT LOOK AT ALL FRIENDLY...

WE'RE OUTNUMBERED. LET'S GO – QUICKLY!

ON 16TH JANUARY, MY TWO SHIPS HEADED OUT INTO THE OPEN OCEAN.

THE WINDS BLEW US EAST, TOWARDS HOME.

WE MADE GOOD SPEED AS THE WINDS STRENGTHENED.

BRRR, IT'S COLD!

ANYTHING WOULD FEEL COLD AFTER THAT PLACE.

WE MADE IT SAFELY BACK ACROSS THE SARGASSO SEA. THIS TIME THE MEN WEREN'T SO NERVOUS.

BUT ON 12TH FEBRUARY, WE WERE **HIT** BY A **VIOLENT STORM**. TWO DAYS PASSED BEFORE THE WINDS EASED. WE **LOST SIGHT** OF THE PINTA.

THEN ON 15TH FEBRUARY, A LOOKOUT SIGHTED LAND.

LAND TO THE SOUTHWEST!

BRING HER ABOUT.

IT WAS SANTA MARÍA, ONE OF THE AZORES ISLANDS.

WE'RE **SAVED**.

THANK HEAVENS!

WE SPENT SEVERAL DAYS THERE BEFORE CONTINUING OUR JOURNEY ON 24TH FEBRUARY.

TWO DAYS LATER, ANOTHER STORM HIT. IT WAS *EVEN WORSE* THAN THE FIRST ONE.*

WE'LL NEVER MAKE IT!

HOLD YOUR COURSE.

*COLUMBUS RETURNED TO EUROPE DURING ONE OF THE WORST WINTERS IN RECORDED HISTORY.

ON 4TH MARCH, WE SAW LAND...

LAND AHOY!

WAVE AFTER WAVE STRUCK MY LITTLE SHIP. THE WINDS WERE SO *FIERCE* THAT THEY *SPLIT* MOST OF THE SAILS. IT WAS ALMOST *IMPOSSIBLE* TO STEER.

IT WAS THE COAST OF PORTUGAL.

THE NIÑA CAN'T TAKE MUCH MORE OF THIS STORM. WE'LL HAVE TO TAKE SHELTER HERE.

NOT LONG AFTER WE ANCHORED, I WAS CALLED TO A MEETING WITH KING JOHN II.

26

RELATIONS BETWEEN PORTUGAL AND SPAIN WERE NOT GOOD. I **FEARED** KING JOHN WOULD THROW ME IN JAIL WHEN I TOLD HIM MY NEWS.

YOUR HIGHNESS, I HAVE FOUND A **WESTERN ROUTE** TO THE INDIES. I CLAIMED MANY NEW LANDS FOR SPAIN.*

*COLUMBUS STILL HOPED THAT HISPANIOLA WAS JAPAN AND BELIEVED THAT CUBA WAS PART OF MAINLAND CHINA.

SURELY YOU **MUST** HAVE HAD TO SAIL THROUGH **PORTUGUESE** WATERS.

NO, MY LORD. WE DID NOT TRAVEL SOUTH OF THE CANARIES.

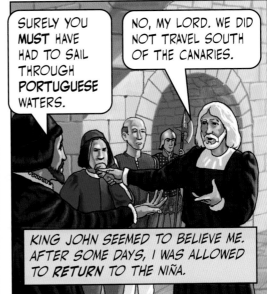

KING JOHN SEEMED TO BELIEVE ME. AFTER SOME DAYS, I WAS ALLOWED TO **RETURN** TO THE NIÑA.

ON 15TH MARCH 1493, I ENTERED PALOS, THE SPANISH PORT I HAD LEFT ALMOST 32 WEEKS EARLIER...

IT'S THE NIÑA!

A FEW HOURS LATER, THE PINTA APPEARED IN THE SAME HARBOUR.*

*THE PINTA HAD SURVIVED THE STORM AND REACHED SPAIN BEFORE COLUMBUS. BUT MARTÍN PINZÓN HAD ANCHORED FOR REPAIRS BEFORE SAILING ON TO PALOS. HE DIED SOON AFTER LANDING.

I WAS INVITED TO COURT. FERDINAND AND ISABELLA WERE KIND ENOUGH TO **HONOUR** THEIR PROMISE TO ME OF TITLES AND OTHER REWARDS.

I SHOWED THEM THE **GOLD** AND OTHER **TREASURES** I HAD FOUND AND THE NATIVES I HAD CAPTURED.

THE SECOND VOYAGE, 1493–1496

THE SPANISH KING AND QUEEN WERE HAPPY TO FUND A **SECOND VOYAGE.** COLUMBUS WAS ORDERED TO CLAIM MORE LANDS, TO BUILD MORE SETTLEMENTS, AND TO BRING CHRISTIANITY TO THE NATIVES. HE LEFT ON 25TH SEPTEMBER, 1493, WITH 17 SHIPS AND ABOUT 1,200 SAILORS AND SETTLERS – INCLUDING HIS BROTHER DIEGO.

ON SUNDAY NOVEMBER 3, WE REACHED A NEW ISLAND IN THE INDIES.* IT WAS THE FIRST OF MANY NEW DISCOVERIES.

THERE'S EVIDENCE OF CANNIBALISM.

*DOMINICA, AN ISLAND IN THE LESSER ANTILLES.

THE NATIVES OF THESE ISLANDS WERE **CARIBS.** THEY WERE WARLIKE AND DID NOT WELCOME US.

THEY'RE FIERCE, EVEN WHEN **CAPTURED.**

ON THE ISLAND I NAMED ST. CROIX, MY MEN ENGAGED IN THEIR FIRST BATTLE IN THE NEW WORLD – AGAINST THE CARIBS.

PANG

AARGH!

WE REACHED OUR FORT, LA NAVIDAD, AT THE END OF NOVEMBER.

THERE'S NO REPLY.

THEY'RE ALL **DEAD!**

HE SAYS SOME TAÍNOS DID IT. THEY WERE LED BY A CHIEFTAIN CALLED CAONABÓ.

I ORDERED A NEW SETTLEMENT TO BE BUILT NEARBY. I NAMED IT **ISABELA,** AFTER THE QUEEN. BUT THINGS WENT **BADLY,** ALMOST FROM THE **START.**

MANY PEOPLE ARE DYING FROM A **STRANGE FEVER.***

SLAP

IN APRIL 1494, I LEFT DIEGO IN CHARGE WHILE I HEADED OFF TO EXPLORE.

KEEP A TIGHT GRIP ON THINGS.

*THE FEVER WAS MALARIA, AND IT WAS SPREAD BY MOSQUITOES.

AFTER EXPLORING MORE OF CUBA AND DISCOVERING JAMAICA, I RETURNED TO FIND HISPANIOLA IN **CHAOS**...

BROTHER BARTOLOMEO! YOU HAVE ARRIVED.

IT IS GOOD TO SEE YOU, CHRISTOPHER. BUT OUR BROTHER HAS HAD **DIFFICULTIES** IN YOUR ABSENCE.

WHAT HAPPENED?

NO ONE WOULD DO ANY WORK.

THE MEN ARE ROAMING ABOUT HUNTING FOR GOLD. THEY'RE **STEALING** FOOD AND TAÍNOS WOMEN.

THE TAÍNOS MEN ARE STARTING TO **FIGHT BACK**.

I'LL HAVE TO STAMP THIS OUT – AND **QUICKLY**.

I ORDERED MY MEN TO HUNT DOWN THE TAÍNOS.*

PANG

*THE SPANIARDS BROUGHT THE FIRST GUNS AND HORSES TO THE AMERICAS. THEY ALSO HAD LARGE, FIERCE DOGS.

AROUND 1,500 TAÍNOS WERE **CAPTURED** AND TAKEN BACK TO SPAIN FOR SALE AS **SLAVES**.

MY MEN EVEN MANAGED TO **TRICK** CHIEF CAONABÓ INTO PUTTING ON **HANDCUFFS**.

OUR KING WEARS THEM ON SPECIAL OCCASIONS. WOULD YOU LIKE TO TRY THEM ON?

BUT MY TROUBLES WEREN'T OVER. SOME OF MY OWN SETTLERS HAD SENT LETTERS TO SPAIN, **COMPLAINING** ABOUT CONDITIONS IN ISABELA.

IN OCTOBER 1495, A GOVERNMENT OFFICIAL ARRIVED FROM SPAIN TO **LOOK INTO THE** COMPLAINTS.

I DECIDED TO RETURN HOME TO DEFEND MY ACTIONS. I LEFT BARTOLOMEO IN CHARGE OF ISABELA. I SET SAIL ON 10TH MARCH, 1496.

THE THIRD VOYAGE, 1498–1500

ALTHOUGH FERDINAND AND ISABELLA WERE CONCERNED ABOUT EVENTS IN HISPANIOLA, THEY HAD NOT LOST FAITH IN COLUMBUS. THEY AGREED TO A *THIRD VOYAGE*. THREE SHIPS TOOK SUPPLIES DIRECTLY TO HISPANIOLA. COLUMBUS TOOK THREE OTHER SHIPS TO EXPLORE REPORTS THAT THE MAINLAND OF CATHAY LAY ON A MORE SOUTHERLY ROUTE.

MY SHIPS LEFT SPAIN ON 30TH MAY, 1498. TWO MONTHS LATER, WE FIRST SIGHTED THE ISLAND I NAMED TRINIDAD.

WHILE EXPLORING THE COAST, WE SUDDENLY HEARD A DREADFUL, ROARING SOUND...

HUH?

...THE BIGGEST WAVE I HAD EVER SEEN RUSHED TOWARDS US. I THOUGHT WE WOULD BE *DESTROYED*!

WE'LL BE SWAMPED!

SAINTS SAVE US!

LUCKILY, IT DID NOT HARM MY THREE SHIPS.

A FEW DAYS LATER, I *DISCOVERED* ANOTHER NEW ISLAND.*

I NAME THIS LAND ISLA DE GRACIA.

*COLUMBUS HAD LANDED ON THE COAST OF WHAT IS NOW VENEZUELA. HE WAS THE FIRST EUROPEAN TO SET FOOT IN SOUTH AMERICA.

ON 15TH AUGUST, I GAVE THE ORDER TO HEAD FOR HISPANIOLA.

MAKE THE COURSE NORTHWEST BY WEST.

I HOPED TO FIND THAT A NEW AND BETTER SETTLEMENT HAD BEEN BUILT TO REPLACE ISABELA.

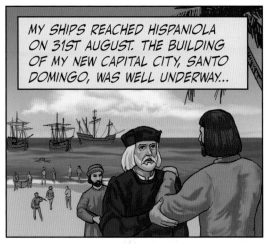

MY SHIPS REACHED HISPANIOLA ON 31ST AUGUST. THE BUILDING OF MY NEW CAPITAL CITY, SANTO DOMINGO, WAS WELL UNDERWAY...

...BUT MY PROBLEMS WITH THE SETTLERS WERE NOT OVER.

WHAT HAPPENED, BARTOLOMEO?

FRANCISCO ROLDÁN LED A **REBELLION**.

I MANAGED TO RESTORE PEACE FOR A WHILE. I PROMISED EACH REBEL A PLOT OF LAND AND TAÍNOS SLAVES TO WORK IT.

BUT THE PEACE DID NOT LAST LONG. I WROTE TO FERDINAND AND ISABELLA, ASKING THEM TO SEND A GOVERNMENT OFFICIAL TO HELP SORT OUT THE SITUATION.

FRANCISCO DE BOBADILLA ARRIVED ON 23RD AUGUST, 1500 – JUST AS **ANOTHER** REBELLION BROKE OUT!

BOBADILLA WAS NOT IMPRESSED. HE **ARRESTED** ME AND MY BROTHERS AND **THREW US IN JAIL**.

IN EARLY OCTOBER, WE WERE SENT HOME TO SPAIN. **I WAS IN CHAINS!**

YOU ARE CHARGED WITH **MISTREATING** THE SETTLERS AND WITHHOLDING GOLD FROM THE CROWN. YOU WILL BE TRIED IN SPAIN.

FORTUNATELY, FERDINAND AND ISABELLA TOOK MY SIDE. AS SOON AS I REACHED SPAIN IN NOVEMBER, **THEY FREED ME**.

THE FOURTH VOYAGE, 1502–1504

FERDINAND AND ISABELLA SAID COLUMBUS COULD LEAD **ONE MORE VOYAGE**. SINCE HE HAD DONE SUCH A POOR JOB RULING HISPANIOLA, THEY MADE NICOLÁS DE OVANDO ITS GOVERNOR. THEY FORBADE COLUMBUS FROM STOPPING IN HISPANIOLA UNLESS HE NEEDED SUPPLIES OR HAD AN EMERGENCY.

I SET SAIL ON 9TH MAY, 1502, WITH FOUR SHIPS. BARTOLOMEO AND MY YOUNGEST SON, FERNANDO, CAME WITH ME.

WE REACHED SANTO DOMINGO ON 29TH JUNE. THE NEW GOVERNOR'S SHIPS WERE READY TO LEAVE FOR SPAIN.

THERE'S A **HURRICANE** COMING. WE NEED TO BE IN THE HARBOUR.

WARN DE OVANDO ABOUT THE STORM, AND ASK IF WE CAN ANCHOR IN THE PORT.

TELL HIM TO KEEP HIS SHIPS IN PORT – IT'S FAR TOO **DANGEROUS** TO SET SAIL.

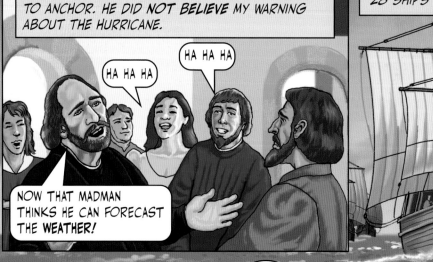

BUT DE OVANDO **REFUSED** TO ALLOW MY SHIPS TO ANCHOR. HE DID **NOT BELIEVE** MY WARNING ABOUT THE HURRICANE.

HA HA HA

HA HA HA

NOW THAT MADMAN THINKS HE CAN FORECAST THE **WEATHER**!

DE OVANDO ORDERED 28 SHIPS TO SEA...

THE HURRICANE *TORE* INTO THE GOVERNOR'S SHIPS. HUNDREDS OF MEN *DROWNED*, INCLUDING BOBADILLA AND ROLDÁN. ONLY ONE SHIP MADE IT BACK TO SPAIN.

BY THE TIME THE HURRICANE HIT MY FOUR SHIPS, WE HAD MADE ANCHOR OFF THE COAST TO THE WEST OF SANTO DOMINGO.

DE OVANDO SHOULD HAVE GIVEN US **SAFE** HARBOUR.

SNAP

ALL SHIPS BUT MY OWN WERE **DRIVEN OUT** TO SEA...

MY CREWS AND I HAD AGREED TO A MEETING PLACE IN CASE OUR SHIPS WERE SEPARATED.

BY SAN FERNANDO – HERE COMES BARTOLOMEO. ALL THE SHIPS ARE **SAFE**!

DUE TO MY MEN'S SKILLFUL SAILING, WE HAD ALL *SURVIVED* THE HURRICANE.

WE HAD TO MAKE REPAIRS, BUT THERE WAS ALSO TIME TO GO FISHING...

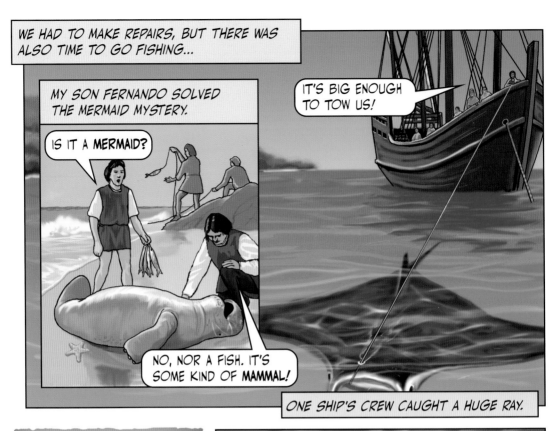

MY SON FERNANDO SOLVED THE MERMAID MYSTERY.

IS IT A **MERMAID**?

NO, NOR A FISH. IT'S SOME KIND OF **MAMMAL!**

IT'S BIG ENOUGH TO TOW US!

ONE SHIP'S CREW CAUGHT A HUGE RAY.

BY 1502, OTHER EXPLORERS HAD VISITED THE SOUTH AMERICAN COAST. THEY SAID IT WAS AN UNKNOWN CONTINENT, AND CALLED IT THE **NEW WORLD**. COLUMBUS BELIEVED THAT CUBA WAS A PENINSULA JOINED TO MAINLAND CHINA. HE HOPED THAT BY EXPLORING THE SEAS TO ITS WEST, HE WOULD FIND A **STRAIT**, OR SEA PASSAGE TO THE INDIAN OCEAN.

ON 30TH JULY, WE SIGHTED A NEW ISLAND.

THESE PEOPLE'S CLOTHES AND WEAPONS ARE BETTER MADE THAN ANY I HAVE YET SEEN.

I NAMED IT BONACCA. FROM IT, WE COULD SEE A HUGE LANDMASS. IT WOULD BE OUR NEXT STOP.

WE ANCHORED OFF A RIVER MOUTH. ON 17TH AUGUST, I CLAIMED THE LAND FOR SPAIN.*

*CHRISTOPHER HAD LANDED IN CENTRAL AMERICA, IN WHAT IS NOW HONDURAS.

YOU COULD GET A HEN'S EGG THROUGH THE HOLE IN HIS EAR!

34

I CONTINUED MY SEARCH FOR A STRAIT. FOR A WHOLE MONTH, WE SUFFERED *DRIVING RAIN* AND *FIERCE WINDS*.

UP WITH THE HELM! EASY NOW!

IT WAS TOO WET TO LIGHT FIRES TO COOK HOT MEALS. OUR FOOD WAS FULL OF *MAGGOTS*.

EURGH!

THE STORM ENDED *AT LAST*...

...BUT TWO OF MY MEN *DROWNED*, ROWING ASHORE FOR FIREWOOD.

IN OCTOBER 1502, WE LANDED IN A *HUGE BAY*. WE TRADED WITH THE NATIVES FOR THEIR MAGNIFICENT GOLD JEWELLERY. USING SIGN LANGUAGE, WE TRIED TO FIND OUT WHETHER THEY KNEW OF A STRAIT TO THE WEST.

HE SEEMS TO BE DESCRIBING A GREAT OCEAN. THE PASSAGE TO IT LIES TO THE *SOUTH*.

OUR SHIPS FOUND A NARROW STRAIT. MY *HOPES* WERE HIGH AS WE SAILED THROUGH IT...

...BUT WE ENDED UP IN YET *ANOTHER* HUGE BAY.

ALL WAS NOT LOST. WE SPENT 10 DAYS THERE, TRADING WITH THE NATIVES FOR GOLD.

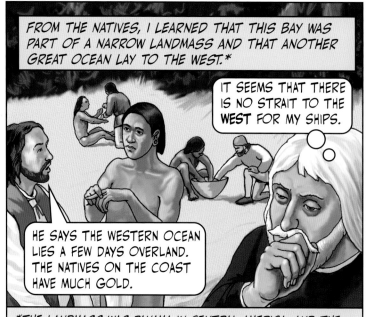

FROM THE NATIVES, I LEARNED THAT THIS BAY WAS PART OF A NARROW LANDMASS AND THAT ANOTHER GREAT OCEAN LAY TO THE WEST.*

IT SEEMS THAT THERE IS NO STRAIT TO THE **WEST** FOR MY SHIPS.

HE SAYS THE WESTERN OCEAN LIES A FEW DAYS OVERLAND. THE NATIVES ON THE COAST HAVE MUCH GOLD.

*THE LANDMASS WAS PANAMA IN CENTRAL AMERICA, AND THE OCEAN WAS THE PACIFIC. COLUMBUS STILL THOUGHT HE WAS IN THE INDIES, ON A PENINSULA JOINED TO MAINLAND CHINA. HE ALSO THOUGHT THAT THE OCEAN TO THE WEST WAS THE INDIAN OCEAN.

INSTEAD OF **WASTING** MORE TIME LOOKING FOR THE **STRAIT**, I'D BE BETTER OFF **HUNTING FOR GOLD.**

WE LEFT THE BAY TO EXPLORE MORE OF THE COASTLINE.

WE ANCHORED OFF A RIVER MOUTH. THEN ON 20TH OCTOBER, I SENT BOATS ASHORE TO TRADE FOR GOLD.

MY MEN WERE MET BY MORE THAN 100 NATIVES, CARRYING SPEARS.

WE COME IN **PEACE.**

WE **CALMED** THE NATIVES DOWN AND DID SOME TRADING. WHEN WE RETURNED THE NEXT DAY, THE NATIVES WERE EVEN **FIERCER.** MY MEN **FIRED** THEIR WEAPONS, WOUNDING ONE OF THE NATIVES. AFTER THIS SHOW OF FORCE, THEY **RAN AWAY.**

BANG

36

WE CONTINUED ALONG THE COAST, BUT FOUND FEW PLACES WHERE WE COULD LAND. THEN IN EARLY NOVEMBER, A STORM BLEW US INTO A GOOD HARBOUR.

I SHALL CALL THIS PLACE PORTO BELLO.

WE STAYED A WEEK, BUT IT WAS WINDY AND WET, DAY AFTER DAY...

WILL THIS RAIN **NEVER** END?

WE LEFT, BUT THE BAD WEATHER CONTINUED. FIERCE WINDS BLEW US BACK UP THE COAST.

ON 13TH DECEMBER, MY MEN WERE **TERRIFIED** BY A BIG **SPOUT** OF MOVING WATER. I CALMED THEM BY TRACING A CROSS IN THE SKY.

FEAR NOT, IT SHALL PASS.

SAINTS SAVE US! IT WILL SINK US ALL!

THE FOUL WEATHER CONTINUED. OUR FOOD SUPPLIES WERE GETTING **LOWER AND LOWER.** EVEN THE **MAGGOTS** ATE BETTER THAN WE DID!

WAIT UNTIL DARK. THAT WAY YOU **WON'T SEE** WHAT YOU'RE EATING.

ON 6TH JANUARY, 1503, MY SHIPS ARRIVED OFF A RIVER I NAMED THE BELÉN. WE SAILED OVER A SAND BAR AND ANCHORED IN THE RIVER MOUTH.

WE'LL STAY HERE FOR A WHILE AND SEARCH FOR GOLD. PERHAPS WE'LL FIND SOME UPRIVER.

THE NATIVES WERE FRIENDLY, AND ALLOWED US TO EXPLORE THE RIVERS.

LOOK – THE WATER IS FULL OF GOLD!

THE REGION WAS FAR RICHER IN GOLD THAN HISPANIOLA.

I DECIDED TO BUILD A SETTLEMENT THERE.

WE'LL NAME IT SANTA MARÍA DE BELÉN.

BUT SOME NATIVES BECAME WARLIKE WHEN THEY REALISED WE PLANNED TO STAY.

THERE ARE 1,000 WARRIORS CAMPED NEARBY ON THE COAST.

MY MEN CAPTURED THE LOCAL CHIEFTAIN, BUT WE COULD NOT HOLD HIM LONG.

ARGH!

HE'S ESCAPED!

ON 6TH APRIL, 1503, I WAS MAKING READY TO SAIL FOR SPAIN WITH THREE SHIPS. THE CREW OF THE FOURTH WAS TO STAY AT OUR SETTLEMENT.

CAPTAIN DIEGO TRISTÁN! WE NEED MORE WATER. TAKE A BOAT OVER THE SANDBAR AND GET SOME.

YES, ADMIRAL.

WHAT THE —?!

THE INDIANS ARE ATTACKING!

SET THE DOGS ON THEM.

PANG

AARGH!

AAAIIE!

THE BATTLE LASTED 3 HOURS, BUT MY SETTLERS WON IN THE END.

DIEGO, WHERE ARE YOU GOING?

UPRIVER, TO GET WATER.

TAKE CARE. THEY MAY ATTACK AGAIN.

AMBUSH!

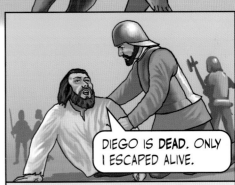

DIEGO IS DEAD. ONLY I ESCAPED ALIVE.

IT WAS DAYS BEFORE I GOT THE SURVIVING SETTLERS SAFELY OFFSHORE. I HAD TO ABANDON MY FOURTH SHIP. THE WEATHER WAS TOO BAD TO GET IT ACROSS THE SAND BAR.

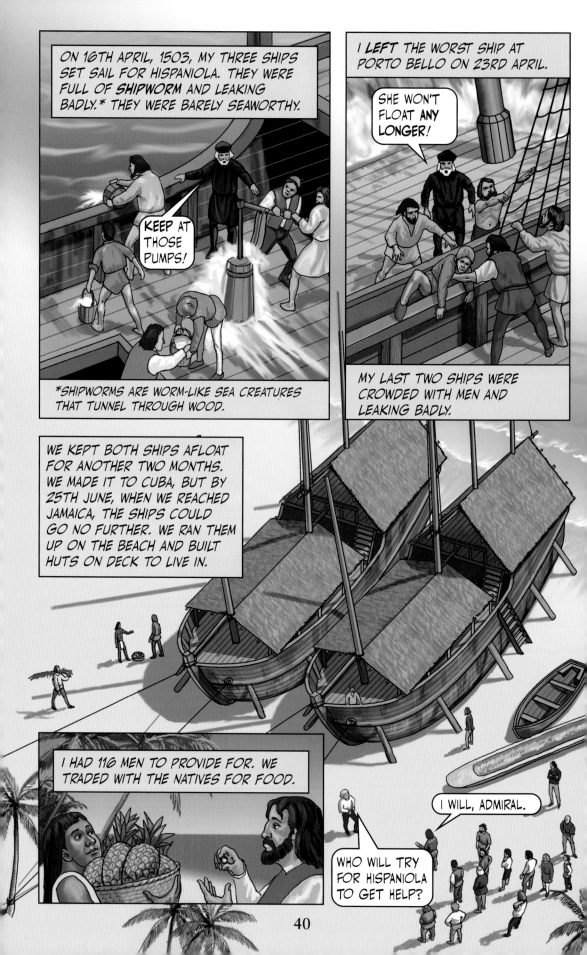

ON 16TH APRIL, 1503, MY THREE SHIPS SET SAIL FOR HISPANIOLA. THEY WERE FULL OF **SHIPWORM** AND LEAKING BADLY.* THEY WERE BARELY SEAWORTHY.

KEEP AT THOSE PUMPS!

*SHIPWORMS ARE WORM-LIKE SEA CREATURES THAT TUNNEL THROUGH WOOD.

I **LEFT** THE WORST SHIP AT PORTO BELLO ON 23RD APRIL.

SHE WON'T FLOAT **ANY** LONGER!

MY LAST TWO SHIPS WERE CROWDED WITH MEN AND LEAKING BADLY.

WE KEPT BOTH SHIPS AFLOAT FOR ANOTHER TWO MONTHS. WE MADE IT TO CUBA, BUT BY 25TH JUNE, WHEN WE REACHED JAMAICA, THE SHIPS COULD GO NO FURTHER. WE RAN THEM UP ON THE BEACH AND BUILT HUTS ON DECK TO LIVE IN.

I HAD 116 MEN TO PROVIDE FOR. WE TRADED WITH THE NATIVES FOR FOOD.

WHO WILL TRY FOR HISPANIOLA TO GET HELP?

I WILL, ADMIRAL.

THAT **BRAVE MAN** WAS CAPTAIN DIEGO MÉNDEZ. WE FITTED TWO DUGOUT CANOES WITH SAILS. A CREW OF SIX SPANIARDS AND TEN NATIVES WAS ON EACH BOAT.

THEY LEFT IN MID-JULY.

THE REST OF US COULD ONLY WAIT AND HOPE. BY 2ND JANUARY, 1504, THERE WAS NO SIGN OF A RESCUE. SOME OF THE MEN WERE **DESPERATE.** THEY **ROSE UP** AGAINST ME.

I'M FOR GOING HOME! WHO IS WITH ME?

WE'RE WITH YOU.

LAID LOW WITH ILLNESS, I WAS **UNABLE** TO STOP THE 50 OR SO REBELS FROM LEAVING.

THEY TOOK TEN CANOES AND TRIED TO ROW TO HISPANIOLA. WHEN THEY FAILED, THEY TOOK OUT THEIR ANGER ON THE NATIVES.

MEANWHILE, THE MEN WHO HAD STAYED LOYAL TO ME AND I FOUND OURSELVES RUNNING LOW ON FOOD. THE NATIVES NO LONGER WISHED TO TRADE WITH US. I FOUND A **SOLUTION** TO THE PROBLEM IN ONE OF MY **PRECIOUS BOOKS.**

HMMM...**THIS** WILL PUT **FEAR** INTO THESE NATIVES!

USING MY BOOK, I WAS ABLE TO WORK OUT THAT THE NEXT *ECLIPSE OF THE MOON* WOULD FALL ON 29TH FEBRUARY.

SAVE US!

IT'S TRUE! THE LIGHT HAS GONE!

MY GOD WILL **PUNISH** YOU UNLESS YOU HELP US.

TO SHOW HIS POWER, HE WILL **PUT OUT** THE MOON'S LIGHT TONIGHT.

OUR HOPES OF RESCUE WERE RAISED IN LATE MARCH 1504...

LOOK — A SHIP!

WELCOME!

DIEGO MÉNDEZ MADE IT TO HISPANIOLA. I CARRY A MESSAGE FROM HIM.

HE'LL **SEND HELP** AS SOON AS HE FINDS A SHIP. GOVERNOR DE OVANDO HAS **FORBIDDEN** ME TO TAKE YOU ON MINE.

DE OVANDO WANTED ME TO **SWEAT IT OUT** A WHILE LONGER. THE MESSENGER LEFT THAT NIGHT.

THE SHIP WAS **TOO SMALL** TO TAKE US ALL. ANOTHER ONE WILL COME **SOON**.

I HID THE TRUTH FROM MY MEN.

I SENT TWO MEN TO THE REBELS' CAMP TO TRY TO SETTLE OUR DIFFERENCES. THE ATTEMPT **FAILED**.

WE GOT NOWHERE, SO WE LEFT THEM.

MY PATIENCE WAS AT AN END. I SENT MY BROTHER BARTOLOMEO AND ALL 50 OF THE OTHER MEN WHO HAD REMAINED LOYAL TO ME TO DEAL WITH THE REBELS...

MERCY! I SURRENDER!

AARRGH

MY LOYAL FRIENDS DEFEATED THE REBELS AND PUT THE RINGLEADER IN CHAINS.

THE RESCUE SHIP ARRIVED IN LATE JUNE.

THANK HEAVENS.

WE LEFT ON 29TH JUNE, 1504. WE HAD BEEN IN JAMAICA FOR JUST OVER ONE YEAR. OUR FIRST STOP WAS HISPANIOLA.

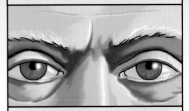

WE CHANGED SHIP THERE, AND SET SAIL FOR SPAIN ON 12TH SEPTEMBER. MY SON FERNANDO AND BROTHER BARTOLOMEO TRAVELLED WITH ME.

WE ARRIVED HOME ON 7TH NOVEMBER, 1504. MY LAST VOYAGE WAS AT AN END.

QUEEN ISABELLA DIED A FEW DAYS AFTER COLUMBUS LANDED. HE NEVER AGAIN VISITED THE SPANISH COURT. HE TRIED, BUT FAILED TO PERSUADE KING FERDINAND TO RESTORE HIS POSITION AS GOVERNOR OF THE INDIES. COLUMBUS'S VOYAGES HAD LEFT HIM RICH IN GOLD BUT POOR IN HEALTH. THE ADMIRAL OF THE OCEAN DIED ON 20TH MAY, 1506. TO THE END, HE WAS SURE THAT HE HAD SUCCEEDED IN REACHING THE INDIES.

THE END

AROUND THE WORLD

*C*olumbus was not the first European to land in the Americas. Viking explorers had achieved this when they sailed to North America in the eleventh century. By 1492, however, these Viking voyages had long been forgotten. Columbus was still the first European to set foot in Central and South America.*

THE UNKNOWN CONTINENTS
Columbus died without realising that he had discovered lands previously unknown to Europeans. He had also pioneered a sea route west across the Atlantic Ocean. The thrilling stories of his travels inspired other explorers to follow in his wake. In 1499-1502, the Italian-born explorer Amerigo Vespucci made two voyages along the

AMERIGO VESPUCCI
Vespucci was the first person to call the Americas the New World. The continents were named after him – America is Latin for Amerigo.

northeastern coast of South America. Unlike Columbus, Vespucci did not think he had reached the Indies. He realised that he had come across an unknown continent, and he named it the New World.

VASCO NÚÑEZ DE BALBOA
In 1513, the Spanish explorer Vasco Núñez de Balboa became the first European to walk across the Americas and see the eastern Pacific Ocean.

SPANISH COLONISATION
In the early sixteenth century, Spanish explorers pushed through North, Central, and South America. Native lands were captured by force and Spanish colonies were founded throughout the New World.

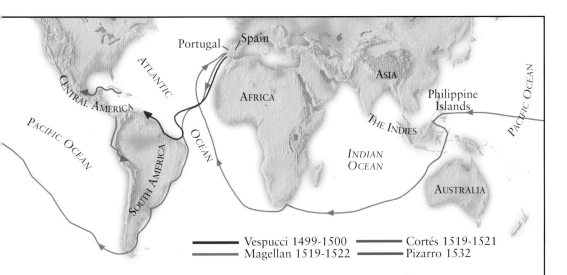

Vespucci 1499-1500   Cortés 1519-1521
Magellan 1519-1522   Pizarro 1532

SAILING WESTWARD TO THE INDIES

Explorers came to realise that they needed to sail around the New World to find a westward route to the Indies. The man who achieved this was Ferdinand Magellan of Portugal. In September 1519, he set sail from Spain with five ships and about 240 men. Just over a year later, his ships entered the strait at the southern tip of South America. One ship was wrecked in it, and another turned back to Spain. It took the three remaining ships almost four months to cross the Pacific Ocean to the Philippine Islands. Magellan was killed there in April 1521. The expedition reached the Indies, but only one ship, the *Vittoria*, and 18 men made it back to Spain. They had completed the first around-the-world voyage.

MAPPING THE WORLD
Before the voyages of the fifteenth and sixteenth centuries, Europeans had little knowledge of the true shape and size of the oceans and continents.

FERDINAND MAGELLAN
Although Magellan did not live to complete it, his 1519-1522 expedition gave the first real proof that the Earth is round.

GLOSSARY

admiral The highest rank in many navies.

cannibal A person who eats human flesh.

chaos Total confusion.

convert To win someone over to another religion or set of ideas.

current The movement of water in a river or an ocean.

eclipse In an eclipse of the moon, the Earth comes between the sun and the moon so that all or part of the moon's light is blocked out.

engage To become busy and occupied doing something.

extraordinary Very unusual or remarkable.

hammock A piece of strong cloth or net that is hung up by each end and used as a bed.

helm A wheel or handle used to steer a boat.

hold The place in a ship where cargo is stored.

interpreter Someone who translates a foreign language, explaining the meaning of words.

landmass A large area of land.

lentils The round seeds of a plant related to beans and peas.

maggot The larva of an insect.

malaria A disease spread to humans by mosquito bites. Victims suffer attacks of chills and fever.

monastery A group of buildings where monks live and work.

Muslims Followers of the religion of Islam. Muslims believe there is only one god. Their holy book is called the Koran.

navigation The science of charting a course for a ship.

peninsula Land that is nearly surrounded by water, but which is still connected to the mainland.

quadrant An instrument used to measure angles, such as those between the stars and the horizon.

ray A type of fish with a flat body, wing-like fins, and a small, whip-like tail.

rebellion A struggle in which people rise up against their leader or ruler.

rebels The people involved in a rebellion.

reef A mass of rock, sand, or coral in shallow water off a coast.

rudder A hinged wood or metal plate attached to the back of a ship. A rudder is used for steering.

trinkets Small worthless objects, such as cheap ornaments or jewellery.

FOR MORE INFORMATION

ORGANISATIONS

The British Museum
Great Russell Street
London
WC1B 3DG
www.thebritishmuseum.ac.uk

National Maritime Museum
Romney Road
Greenwich
London
SE10 9NF
www.nmm.ac.uk

FOR FURTHER READING
If you liked this book, you might also want to try:

Avoid Sailing with Christopher Columbus!
by Fiona Macdonald, Book House, 2004

Avoid being a Tudor Colonist!
by Jacqueline Morley, Book House, 2004

Christopher Columbus (Famous Lives series)
by M. Lacey, Usborne Publishing Ltd, 2004

Explorer (Eyewitness Guides)
by Rupert Matthews, Dorling Kindersley, 2003

12 October 1492: Columbus Reaches America (Dates with History)
by John Malam, Evans Brothers, 2003

INDEX

Websites

Due to the changing nature of internet links, the Salariya Book Company has developed an online list of websites related to the subject of this book. This site is updated regularly. Please use this link to access the list:

http://www.book-house.co.uk/gnf/columbus